CCJC
1/06

WORLD OF

MAMMALS

GIRAFFES

by Sophie Lockwood

Content Adviser: Barbara E. Brown, Associate, Mammal Division, The Field Museum, Chicago, IL

THE CHILD'S WORLD®, CHANHASSEN, MINNESOTA

GIRAFFES

Published in the United States of America by The Child's World®
PO Box 326 • Chanhassen, MN 55317-0326 • 800-599-READ • www.childsworld.com

Acknowledgements:

The Child's World®: Mary Berendes, Publishing Director

Editorial Directions, Inc.: E. Russell Primm, Editorial Director; Pam Rosenberg, Editor; Judith Shiffer, Assistant Editor; Matt Messbarger, Editorial Assistant; Susan Hindman, Copy Editor; Emily Dolbear, Proofreader; Judith Frisbie and Olivia Nellums, Fact Checkers; Tim Griffin/IndexServ, Indexer; Cian Loughlin O'Day, Photo Researcher, Linda S. Koutris, Photo Editor

The Design Lab: Kathleen Petelinsek, Designer, Production Artist, and Cartographer

Photos:

Cover: Tom & Dee Ann McCarthy/Corbis; half title/CIP: Corbis; frontispiece: Getty Images/Stone/Manoj Shah.

Interior: Animals Animals/Earth Scenes: 10 (John Chellman), 20 (Manoj Shah), 29 (Barbara Von Hoffmann), 34 (ABPL Image Library); Corbis: 12 (Jim Zuckerman), 15 (Michele Westmorland) 24 (Kevin Schafer), 30 (Tim Davis); Digital Vision: 5-top right and 16, 5-middle left and 19, 5-bottom right and 23; Getty Images: 7 (AFP/Deshakalyan Chowdhury), 36 (Photographer's Choice/Theo Westernberger); Getty Images/The Image Bank: 5-top left and 8 (Joseph Van Os), 37 (Bill Hickey); Ricki Rosen/Corbis Saba: 5-bottom left and 32.

Library of Congress Cataloging-in-Publication Data

Lockwood, Sophie.
  Giraffes / by Sophie Lockwood.
     p. cm. — (The world of mammals)
  Includes index.
  ISBN 1-59296-496-6 (lib. bdg. : alk. paper) 1. Giraffe—Juvenile literature. I. Title.
II. World of mammals (Chanhassen, Minn.)
  QL737.U56L63 2005
  599.638—dc22   2005000538

TABLE OF CONTENTS

Chapter One

Rescue!

A five-year-old Masai giraffe cow moves away from the herd. She is looking for a good place to give birth to her first calf. She finds a safe clearing among a stand of acacia trees at the edge of Masai Mara National Reserve in Kenya.

She delivers her baby standing up. The calf drops onto its head. Kerplop! Her newborn male giraffe stands a whopping 1.8 meters (6 feet) tall and weighs almost 68 kilograms (150 pounds).

The mother giraffe licks her baby so she can memorize his scent. She keeps an eye on the **savanna.** Nearly half of all newborn giraffes are lost to **predators** during their first month of life. Lions, crocodiles, leopards, hyenas, and African hunting dogs attack young giraffes. Mother, however, can defend her baby. Her hooves are the size of

Would You Believe?
A mother giraffe is pregnant for fourteen to fifteen months. Among mammals, only rhino and elephant mothers carry their babies longer.

This newborn giraffe will stay close to its mother for many months.

dinner plates and can crush a lion's head with one blow.

The young bull calf is on his feet within twenty minutes of his birth. He is wobbly, but standing and walking within a couple of hours. He reaches to drink from his mother's nipple within one hour of his birth. Giraffes, like humans, are mammals and drink milk.

Three days later, a thunderstorm booms over the savanna. Lightning flashes and sends the giraffe and her

Two adult Rothschild's giraffes watch over a calf in Kenya.

Would You Believe?
A baby giraffe nearly doubles its height in a year. Drinking milk and eating leaves, it grows 2.5 to 5 centimeters (1 to 2 inches) a week—about 15 centimeters (6 in) a month.

calf into a panic. Mother dashes through the tall grass with her calf close behind. Through the rain, she does not see the power lines that stretch from pole to pole. She runs into the lines, gets caught, and dies from an electric shock.

A passing ranger sees the dead mother and her young calf standing beside her. Fear fills the young bull and he runs away as the ranger approaches. The ranger calls for help. The baby giraffe can't survive without its mother unless humans help. Capturing the baby without injury will be difficult. It takes professionals to rescue even a small giraffe.

The rescue team arrives. They plan to build a chute and herd the bull calf into a protected corral. They need to **tranquilize** the calf. But the calf is afraid of humans and could kick out and injure a team member or himself. Setting up the chute and the corral takes time. The team has to work quickly. They know that the bull calf needs milk—and needs it fast—if he is to survive.

Finally, the calf runs down the chute and into the corral. A quick injection with the tranquilizing medicine calms the giraffe. He is loaded into a high-sided

Would You Believe?
Every giraffe's skin has its own spot pattern. A giraffe's spots are as unique as human fingerprints.

truck and taken to the nearest wildlife **rehabilitation** center.

It has been nearly ten hours since the mother giraffe died. As soon as they can, the rescue team offers the calf milk from a bottle. The baby giraffe needs to drink about 2 liters (0.5 gallons) of milk six times a day. The team has rescued the orphan calf, but their work is just beginning. They must teach the calf how to be a giraffe—lessons he normally would have learned from his mother. When he is grown and can fend for himself, the bull will be returned to the wild. He'll join a herd, father many calves, and feed among the treetops on the African savanna.

A baby giraffe that has lost its mother must be
fed milk from a bottle in order to survive.

Chapter Two

Long Necks and Big Hearts

Giraffes may be the strangest looking animals on the savanna. They stand as tall as many trees, with necks like building cranes. They have lumpy heads with large eyes and long eyelashes. Giraffes have skinny legs with knobby knees. Their skins have lots and lots of spots. They also have tails that make excellent flyswatters.

Giraffes are herbivores—they eat plants. They are not picky eaters and feed on about one hundred different plants, but they prefer tender acacia leaves to any other plant. An adult giraffe might eat up to 34 kilograms (75 lbs) of leaves a day.

Acacias, however, come equipped to frustrate hungry giraffes. They have thorns that make munching a challenge. A giraffe's 46-centimeter-long (18-in-long) **prehensile** tongue can work its way between the thorns. Its saliva is thick and helps protect the giraffe's tongue from the prickly

thorns. But the whistling thorn acacias have other protec-
tors—stinging ants. After a few nibbles at a tree, the giraffe
will start to feel the stings of the ants. That's how the giraffe
knows it is time to move on to the next tree. That's also
nature's way of protecting the trees from being overeaten.

A giraffe feeds on the leaves of an acacia tree.

A giraffe's stomach has four compartments, each of which plays a part in **digestion.** A giraffe eats his meals more than once. On the first round, he chews enough leaves to form a leaf ball. Once swallowed, the leaf ball returns to the mouth to be chewed again. This is called chewing cud. Then the cud moves into the next chamber. Each chamber helps digest the cud and take nutrition from the food.

LOOOOONG NECKS

A giraffe's neck is about 1.8 meters (6 ft) long—about the height of an adult man. It weighs about 227 kilograms (500 lbs)—the weight of five or six fifth graders.

A flexible neck allows the giraffe to reach the tender leaves of most savanna trees. A giraffe's neck bends easily because of the way its **vertebrae** are connected to one another. The vertebrae connect like hip joints on humans. A ball shape on one vertebra fits into a socket on the next vertebra. Surrounding the vertebrae are strong muscles and thick blood vessels.

Males use their necks for sparring, also called necking. Sparring is fake fighting. Two males line up next to each other and whack each other with their necks.

Would You Believe?
A giraffe has only seven vertebrae in its neck. That's the same number as humans have but a giraffe's vertebrae are much bigger.

The stronger giraffe is the winner, the **dominant** male. Sparring is an important skill because only dominant males get to mate with females. Males mate with many different females. They do not form a bond with just one mate.

A BIG HEART

It takes a good-sized heart to pump enough blood to reach a giraffe's brain. A giraffe's heart weighs about 11 kilograms (24 lbs) and is about 60 centimeters (2 ft) long. This is about the size of a one-year-old child. The heart muscle wall is strong and about 7 centimeters (3 in) thick. A giraffe's heart beats about 170 times per minute—roughly two-and-a-half times faster than a human heart.

The heart pumps blood through veins and arteries that are the same size as the pipes under your bathroom sink. The vessels carrying blood to the brain are specially formed. They have small valves that help push blood toward the giraffe's brain. As the blood passes through the valve, it closes. This stops the blood from falling back to the heart.

Giraffe necks also have an unusual network of blood vessels just before reaching the brain. This network is

*Sparring is an important skill that helps determine which
male giraffes will be allowed to mate with the females.*

called the *rete mirabile*, which means "marvelous network" in Latin. The vessels prevent too much blood from entering or leaving the brain, even when the giraffe bends over or rises quickly. If the giraffe didn't have this special network of blood vessels, it would faint every time it bent to drink water. Bending over is already hard enough for giraffes without passing out into a water hole!

Bending down to drink water is an awkward task for a giraffe!

Chapter Three

Speckled Gigantic Flowers

A giraffe herd is unlike most other animal groups. Giraffes need lots of room, so they tend to have loose, disorganized herds. Unlike a wolf pack or lion pride, a giraffe herd has no leaders. No single animal keeps the others in line or tells the others what to do. In *Out of Africa*, author Isak Dinesen described a giraffe herd moving: "[A group of giraffes] in their queer . . . gracefulness, [move] as if it were not a herd of animals but a family of rare, long-stemmed, speckled gigantic flowers slowly advancing."

A herd contains bulls, cows, and calves. The bulls, taller by about 60 centimeters (2 ft) than the cows, feed off the top tree

Would You Believe?
Giraffes can run at a speed of about 48 kilometers (30 miles) per hour. When a giraffe moves, the legs on one side of its body move forward and then the legs on the other side move forward. This is called pacing.

branches. Cows browse among the lower branches, and calves munch the lowest leaves. Giraffes do not eat grass. A bent-over giraffe is open to attack by predators. It is better to stand tall and chew leaves.

Giraffes feed mostly at sunrise and sunset and rest during the hot afternoons. They need to eat plenty of leaves to keep those huge bodies healthy. Because they eat only a few leaves off each tree, they also spend plenty of time traveling.

So when do giraffes sleep? Giraffes sleep only about two hours a day, and that sleep comes in short ten- to twelve-minute-long naps. Although they can lie down, giraffes usually take naps standing. With lions, leopards, and hyenas around, lying down is not safe. It takes too long to stand up should trouble arise.

Early in the day, the males move away. They do not protect the herd, because females can wallop predators just as well as males. And males don't need to collect food for the young either. Babies drink milk from their mothers and begin eating leaves before they are one month old. Because the bulls' only job is to father more giraffes, the adult males spend most of their time alone.

Mother giraffes drop their calves off

at a kind of giraffe day care. Called a crèche (KRESH), the giraffe nursery has several **offspring** and one mother babysitting them. Mothers stop by every few hours to give their young a drink of milk. Then they leave to find more food.

Giraffe mothers and babies do not bond like baboons or chimpanzees. Mom recognizes her own baby and feeds it when necessary. She does not groom her baby or protect it in any special way. The female in charge of the nursery provides any protection needed. She can kill a lion or leopard with one swipe of her hoof.

Young giraffes are most vulnerable during their first

Many young giraffes do not survive their first year. It is up to adult giraffes to help protect the calves from predators.

Giraffes are tall and have excellent vision, making it unlikely that predators will be able to sneak up on them. That is why other animals, such as these zebras, like to graze near giraffes.

year of life. Danger lurks behind every bush. Only one in four infants reaches the age of one year. By that time, baby has grown to 3.7 meters (12 ft). Giraffes reach their adult height and weight by three or four years old. Once a giraffe is full-sized, the only predators to worry about are human. Giraffes that survive their first year in the wild generally live to be twenty to thirty years old.

Giraffes have been called the sentries of the savanna. They have excellent eyesight and, because they sleep so little, are almost always alert. Their height allows them to see quite far. In addition, their hearing and sense of smell are also very good. This makes it very unlikely that a lion will be able to sneak up on a giraffe. On the open savanna, zebras, antelopes, and wildebeests like to graze near giraffes. The giraffes let other grazers know when danger is hiding in the tall grasses.

Giraffes communicate with their eyes and with sounds. Giraffes have the largest eyes of any land mammal, and they keep in contact with other herd members by watching out for visual signals. For many years, people believed that giraffes were mute. This is not true. Giraffes grunt, moo, bray, moan, and bellow. They just don't do it all the time. Their speech is not loud like a lion's roar or an elephant's trumpeting, but other giraffes can hear and understand it just fine.

Chapter Four

The Giraffe Family Tree

For many years, people thought all giraffes were pretty much the same. No one noticed the differences between Nubian and Masai giraffes, for example. They looked like twins, or at least like brothers and sisters.

While there is only one giraffe **species,** there are nine **subspecies.** They include Masai, Thornicroft's, reticulated, Rothschild's, Nubian, Angolan, Southern, Kordofan, and West African giraffes. Telling one subspecies from another requires a keen eye, a measuring stick, a scale, and a map.

Each giraffe's spot pattern is unique. Among subspecies, shapes, sizes, colors, and locations of the spot patterns differ. But you must look closely because the differences are very small.

Masai (or Kilimanjaro) giraffes have

Would You Believe?
The worldwide population of giraffes is about 141,000. Of those, 50,000 live in protected areas like parks and preserves, and 8,000 live on private land. With only 445 living in the wild, Rothschild's giraffes are the smallest group.

Two Southern giraffes stand next to a water hole.

irregular, star-shaped, or leaf-shaped splotches. They have no spots below their knees. Thornicroft's (Rhodesian) giraffes sport a mix of star-shaped and leaf-shaped spots, but their spots extend to the hoof.

Reticulated (or Somali) giraffes look like a beige net has been thrown over a chocolate or liver-colored background. The spot pattern is rectangular and may cover the lower legs. The background color ranges from dark tan to chocolate brown, and males grow darker with age.

Rothschild's (or Baringo or Ugandan) giraffes have paler, thicker fur with orangey brown rectangular splotches. Like Masai

Take a close look at these giraffes. Can you tell what kind they are? (Answer: Masai giraffes)

giraffes, they have no spots below the knee. Nubians have a similar rectangular pattern of chestnut brown spots with off-white lines in between.

Angolan (or Smoky) giraffes have very large spots with notched edges. The pattern covers head to hoof. Southern giraffes look like Angolan giraffes, since both have star-shaped spots that cover the entire body.

Kordofan giraffes have a smaller, odd-shaped spot pattern that covers even the inner legs. A West African (or Nigerian) giraffe's spots are similar in shape to the Angolan, only yellowish red in color.

SIZE? EXTRA-LARGE!

Male giraffes loom 5 to 5.5 meters (16 to 18 ft) above the ground. Females are about 60 centimeters (2 ft) shorter. Masai giraffes tend to be taller than reticulated giraffes—that's where the measuring stick comes in. Giraffes are so much taller than humans that most people don't see a big difference between a 5-meter (16-ft) reticulated giraffe and a 5.5-meter (18-ft) Masai bull.

Bulls outweigh cows. Masai giraffes usually weigh the most, but giraffe weights cover a wide range. An adult bull weighs anywhere from 773 kilograms (1,700 lbs) to a whopping, car-sized 1,900 kilograms (4,190 lbs). Adult cows also have a wide weight range: 545 to 1,227 kilograms (1,200 to 2,700 lbs).

All giraffes have bony knobs or horns on their heads. Called ossicones, the knobs are made of skin-covered bone. Two ossicones are normal for both males and females, but some giraffes have up to five horns. If a giraffe has five horns, the fifth horn is located in the middle of its forehead. Males use their horns for fighting. Giraffe horns have no sharp points, but can still do damage because they are rock-hard.

WHERE GIRAFFES ARE FOUND

Subspecies	Range
Angolan	Southern Angola, northern Namibia, and western Botswana
Kordofan	Western Sudan
Masai	Southern Kenya and Tanzania
Nubian	Eastern Sudan and Eritrea
Reticulated	Northeastern Kenya, southern Ethiopia, and western Somalia
Rothschild's	Western Kenya and eastern Uganda
Southern	Southeastern Zimbabwe, South Africa, and Mozambique
Thornicroft's	Northern Namibia
West African	Northern Nigeria

All nine giraffe subspecies live on the continent of Africa.

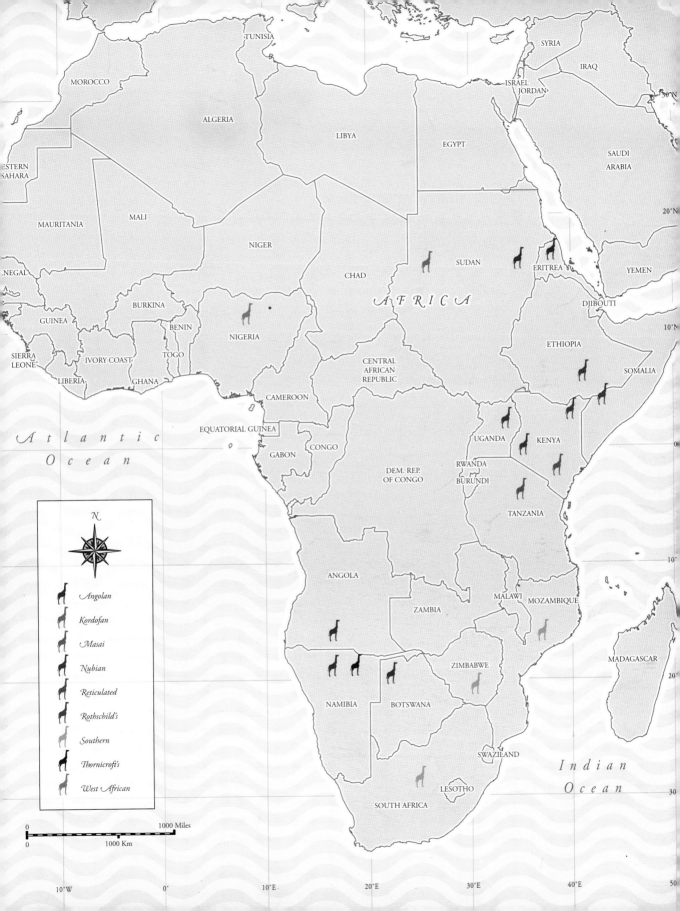

TUNISIA

SYRIA

IRAQ

MOROCCO

ISRAEL
JORDAN

ALGERIA

LIBYA

EGYPT

SAUDI
ARABIA

WESTERN
SAHARA

50 N

MAURITANIA

MALI

20°N

NIGER

SUDAN

ERITREA

YEMEN

SENEGAL

CHAD

A F R I C A

DJIBOUTI

A

BURKINA

GUINEA

BENIN

SIERRA
LEONE

IVORY COAST

TOGO

NIGERIA

CENTRAL
AFRICAN
REPUBLIC

ETHIOPIA

10°N

SOMALIA

LIBERIA

GHANA

CAMEROON

A t l a n t i c

EQUATORIAL GUINEA

UGANDA

KENYA

GABON

CONGO

O c e a n

DEM. REP.
OF CONGO

RWANDA
BURUNDI

0°

TANZANIA

10°

ANGOLA

MALAWI

MOZAMBIQUE

N

ZAMBIA

MADAGASCAR

Angolan

Kordofan

NAMIBIA

ZIMBABWE

20°

Masai

BOTSWANA

Nubian

Reticulated

Rothschild's

Southern

SWAZILAND

I n d i a n

Thornicroft's

LESOTHO

O c e a n

30

West African

SOUTH AFRICA

0   1000 Miles

0   1000 Km

10°W   0°   10°E   20°E   30°E   40°E   50

THE GIRAFFE'S ONLY RELATIVE: THE OKAPI

Giraffes and okapis are cousins, but they look nothing alike. Giraffes are tall and spotted; okapis are short with stripes on their rumps. Giraffes like the open savanna; okapis like dense, damp forests. Giraffes live in loose herds; okapis keep to themselves.

The okapi is a rare animal that looks like a cross between a giraffe, a horse, and a zebra. Its head is the same as a giraffe's head, complete with long tongue and short horns. Its middle is horse shaped and colored. An okapi has stripes on its rump and upper legs like those of a zebra. Its lower legs are white.

The okapi's body measures 1.8 to 2 meters (6 to 7 ft) long, and it stands about 1.5 meters (5 ft) high at the shoulder. They are lightweights compared to their giraffe relatives. Okapis range from about 210 to 250 kilograms (460 to 550 lbs). Three fat okapis weigh as much as one skinny giraffe.

Okapis live in the dense forests of the

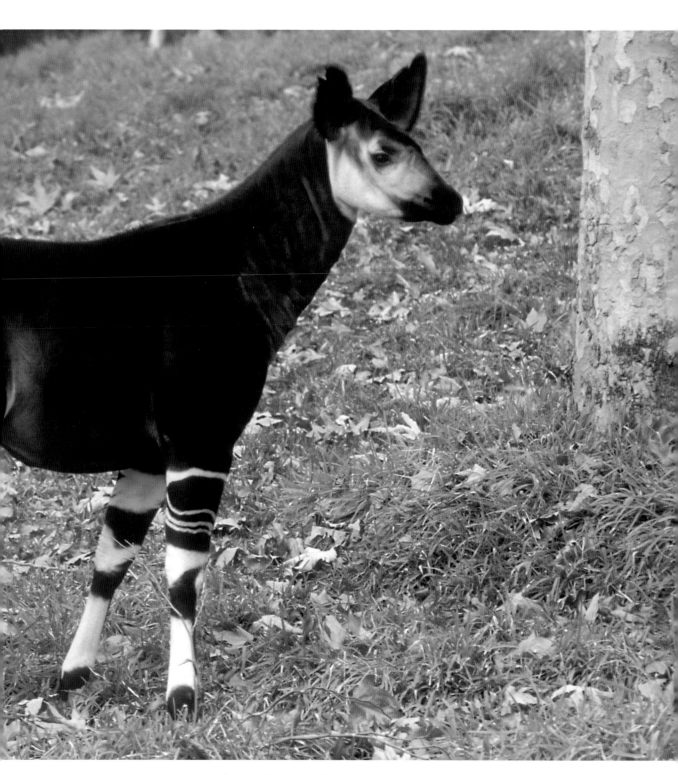

Scientists first discovered the okapi in 1900.

Congo River basin in Africa. Scientists think there may be 10,000 to 25,000 okapis in the wild. No one truly knows because okapis are hard to count. They live by themselves. Heavy tree cover hides the forest floor where the okapi lives. Taking an accurate count of the secretive okapis could take a lifetime!

Okapis live in the dense rain forests of the Congo River Basin in Central Africa.

Chapter Five

The Past, The Present, and The Future

Ten thousand years ago, giraffes spread throughout Africa. Then the climate changed. Over time, the vast, tree-dotted grasslands of the north gave way to desert. Today, giraffes are found only below the Sahara Desert in what is called sub-Saharan Africa.

From the time humans first lived in Africa, giraffes fascinated people. We know this because those early humans carved pictures of giraffes into stone and painted giraffe portraits in caves. In 1997, a larger-than-life carving of giraffes was found on a rock high above the deserts of Niger. Scientists believe the **petroglyph** was made 6,000 to 9,000 years ago. Similar art has been found in South Africa and Namibia. In those cases, cave paintings show giraffes with their heads above the clouds.

Humans often want to keep what nature creates in the wild. That's what a zoo is—a collection of nature's animals.

This Roman mosaic of wild animals, including a giraffe,
was found during a road construction project in Israel.

One of the earliest known zoos was that of Egypt's Queen Hatshepsut. About 3,500 years ago, she had a giraffe brought about 2,400 kilometers (1,500 miles) down the Nile River for her private zoo. Since then, zoos have sought giraffes to put on display.

When Romans brought the first giraffe from Africa to Rome in 46 B.C., people were astonished. They thought the giraffe was a combination of a camel and a leopard. The term they used was *camelopardalis,* which became the official name of the giraffe species.

A giraffe's arrival at the Paris, France, zoo in 1827 caused a near riot. Everyone wanted to see the strange creature. Women began wearing clothes and hairdos modeled after the giraffe. Spots and speckles became very fashionable.

TODAY AND TOMORROW

Giraffes are not endangered or threatened in the wild. Of the nine subspecies, only the Kordofan, West African, and Rothschild's giraffes have small populations. Scientists, aware of the problem, have developed programs to protect these species.

The biggest problem for giraffes is **poaching.** Hunting a giraffe is illegal in most African nations. However, many of the people are poor. Killing one giraffe provides

more money for a family than a year's worth of farming. The tails are sold to make flyswatters and bracelets for tourists. Giraffe skin makes excellent shoes and is a traditional fabric for hunting shields. The meat from a giraffe feeds an entire village for days.

The hunting of giraffes by starving Africans takes it toll. And the growing African population continues to take over giraffe territory. The combination of hunting and habitat loss has eliminated giraffes from Mauritania, Mali, and Senegal.

A group of African men butcher a giraffe they have killed. Sadly, killing one giraffe can provide more money than a year's worth of farming.

Some landowners, however, find that giraffes make excellent companions for cattle or sheep. Giraffes keep tree cover under control by pruning the leaves. They do not compete with cattle or sheep for food. An added bonus of having a giraffe herd on the ranch is their "early warning system." They can see approaching lions, leopards, or other predators. The other animals learn a predator is coming and head to safer territory.

ZOO LIFE

It would be hard to find a zoo that doesn't have a small herd of giraffes. Older zoos kept giraffes in small, crowded cages. Recent advances in zoo management have given giraffes a better life in **captivity.** Open savannas, such as the one at the San Diego Wild Animal Park, provide giraffes a place to roam freely within a park or preserve.

Zoos trade bull giraffes for breeding purposes. It is important that Rothschild's giraffes, for example, breed only with other Rothschild's. That way, the subspecies can be preserved. But think about the problems of shipping a giraffe from Washington, D.C., to Boston. Suppose the bull is 5.5 meters (18 ft) tall. What do you put him in for shipping? If you put him in a tall cage on a truck bed, you can't drive on the highway. He won't fit under the bridges,

and you'd need to watch out for trees and power lines. Similar problems exist with trains and airplanes. Shipping requires careful planning, well-mapped routes, and plenty of time to travel safely.

Zoo-to-zoo breeding programs are a success. New baby giraffes attract attention at zoos throughout the world. Children line up to see the calves munch leaves and drink mother's milk. Kids cringe as the babies clean their ears with their own tongues. Yuck! But baby giraffes

A giraffe at the Tarongo Zoo in Sydney, Australia, looks out over the city's skyline.

do more than entertain. They preserve their species and teach people about giraffes.

As Africa's population continues to grow, giraffes will lose more territory in the wild. Less territory means fewer giraffes can survive. Effective programs to preserve giraffes before they become endangered make sense. With any luck, those children who stared in wonder at the baby calves cleaning their ears with their tongues will join the fight to save this remarkable species.

Giraffe habitats in zoos give many people a chance to see these wonderful animals and observe their behavior.

Glossary

captivity (cap-TIH-vi-tee) the state of living within boundaries, such as in a zoo, preserve, or park

digestion (duh-JESS-chuhn) the process of breaking down food for nutrition

dominant (DOM-uh-nuhnt) the strongest or most powerful

offspring (OFF-spring) the young of a species

parasites (PA-ruh-sites) animals or plants that get food by living on or in another living thing

petroglyph (PET-roh-glif) a carving done in rock

poaching (POH-ching) hunting or fishing illegally

predators (PRED-uh-turz) animals that hunt and kill other animals for food

prehensile (pree-HEN-suhl) made for grabbing or gripping by wrapping around an object

rehabilitation (ree-huh-bil-uh-TAY-shuhn) restoring an individual to its normal life

savanna (suh-VAN-uh) a tropical grassland

species (SPEE-sheez) a group of animals that share certain characteristics

subspecies (SUHB-spee-sheez) a category or type of animal within a species

tranquilize (TRANG-kwuhl-eyez) to make calm by using medication

vertebrae (VUR-tuh-bray) the bones found in the neck and spine

For More Information

Watch It

Tall Blondes, VHS (New York: Thirteen/WNET New York, 2002.)

Read It

Jango-Cohen, Judith. *Giraffes*. New York: Marshall Cavendish/ Benchmark Books, 2002.

Leach, Michael. G*iraffe: Habitats, Life Cycles, Food Chains, Threats*. Austin, Tex.: Raintree Steck-Vaughn, 2001.

Markert, Jenny. *Giraffes*. Chanhassen, Minn.: The Child's World, 2001.

Watt, E. Melanie. *Giraffes*. Austin, Tex.: Raintree Steck-Vaughn, 2002.

Look It Up

Visit our home page for lots of links about giraffes:
http://www.childsworld.com/links

Note to Parents, Teachers, and Librarians: We routinely verify our Web links to make sure they are safe, active sites—so encourage your readers to check them out!

The Animal Kingdom
Where Do Giraffes Fit In?

Kingdom: Animal

Phylum: Chordates (animals with backbones)

Class: Mammalia (animals that feed their young milk)

Order: Artiodactyla (even-toed)

Family: Giraffidae

Genus: *Giraffa*

Species: *camelopardalis*

Subspecies:

angolensis (Angolan)

antiquorum (Kordofan)

camelopardalis (Nubian)

giraffa (Southern)

peralta (West African)

reticulata (reticulated)

rothschildi (Rothschild's)

thornicrofti (Thornicroft's)

tippelskirchi (Masai)

Index

About the Author

Sophie Lockwood is a former teacher and a longtime writer. She writes textbooks, newspaper articles, and magazine articles. Sophie enjoys writing about animals and their habits. The most interesting part of her research, Sophie says, is learning how scientists apply their knowledge to save endangered species. She lives with her husband in the foothills of the Blue Ridge Mountains.